# SANTA FE UNCOVERED

## A LOCAL'S INSIGHT INTO THE HEART OF NEW MEXICO

## KIMBERLY BURK CORDOVA

# CONTENTS

*To the resilient New Mexican Indigenous People, custodians of Santa Fe's ancient wisdom and cultural treasures. This book is dedicated to honoring your enduring spirit and rich heritage, integral to the enchanting tapestry of Santa Fe. May its pages echo the beauty and significance of your legacy, inviting all to appreciate the profound contributions that have shaped this sacred land.*

"Santa Fe is an inspirational place. Its geographical beauty, sheer mountains, visceral colors, pure air, and unending sky make it a magical place for me."

— D.H. LAWRENCE, RENOWNED ENGLISH WRITER

# INTRODUCTION

## OVERVIEW OF SANTA FE'S UNIQUE CHARM

Nestled in the high desert of New Mexico, Santa Fe stands as a beacon of cultural richness and distinct charm. Known as "The City Different," it beckons visitors with its captivating blend of Native American, Spanish, and Anglo influences. The city's unique character is embodied in its adobe architecture, a harmonious marriage of earthy tones, rounded edges, and a history that dates back centuries. This enchanting aesthetic, a vibrant arts scene, and a spiritual energy permeating the air make Santa Fe a destination unlike any other.

## BRIEF HISTORICAL BACKGROUND

Santa Fe's roots delve deep into history, with a lineage predating European settlers' arrival. Established as the Spanish "Kingdom of New Mexico" capital in 1610, Santa Fe is one of the oldest continuously inhabited cities in the United States. The Plaza, a historic epicenter, has witnessed centuries of cultural exchange, trade, and the ebb and flow of diverse communities. The adobe architecture, a legacy of Spanish colonial influence, further contributes to the city's timeless appeal.

## PURPOSE OF THE TRAVEL GUIDE

The purpose of this travel guide is to serve as your compass in navigating the myriad offerings of Santa Fe. Whether you are a first-time visitor or a seasoned traveler returning to this cultural haven, the guide aims to unravel the city's unique tapestry. From uncovering hidden gems cherished by locals to providing insights into the best activities for all age groups, we endeavor to offer a comprehensive and authentic exploration of Santa Fe. Beyond the surface, we will delve into the city's fun facts, trivia, and insider tips, allowing you to experience the essence of Santa Fe beyond the ordinary tourist trail.

Embark on a journey through the historic streets, savor the flavors of Southwestern cuisine, and immerse yourself in the arts and culture that define Santa Fe. As you explore, let this guide be your companion, unveiling the wonders of a city where history, tradition, and creativity converge to create an unforgettable experience. Welcome to Santa Fe, where every step tells a story, and every moment is an opportunity for discovery.

# PRACTICAL INFORMATION

## TIME ZONE AND LOCAL CUSTOMS

### TIME ZONE

Santa Fe, New Mexico, operates on Mountain Standard Time (MST) and follows daylight saving time during the warmer months (from the second Sunday in March to the first Sunday in November). Be sure to check the local time and adjust your schedule accordingly.

### LOCAL CUSTOMS

**Respect for Tradition:** Santa Fe takes pride in its rich cultural heritage. Respect local traditions and customs, especially during religious or cultural events. Engage with the community with an open mind and a willingness to learn about the city's diverse history.

**Cultural Etiquette:** When visiting Native American pueblos or participating in cultural events, adhere to any guidelines provided by the community. Photography restrictions may apply in some sacred regions, so always ask for permission before taking pictures.

**Casual and Relaxed Atmosphere:** The overall atmosphere in Santa Fe is calm and relaxed. Whether exploring art galleries or enjoying outdoor activities, dress comfortably and embrace the laid-back ambiance.

## EMERGENCY CONTACTS

### LOCAL AUTHORITIES

**Police:** In emergencies, dial 911 for immediate assistance from the Santa Fe Police Department.

**Fire Department:** For fire emergencies, call 911 to reach the Santa Fe Fire Department.

### HOSPITALS

**Christus St. Vincent Regional Medical Center:** 455 St. Michael's Drive, Santa Fe, NM. Emergency services are available 24/7.

**Presbyterian Santa Fe Medical Center:** 4801 Beckner Road, Santa Fe, NM. Comprehensive medical services and emergency care.

## EMBASSY

While Santa Fe does not have foreign embassies, the closest international representation is in Albuquerque or other major cities. For consulate information, check with your country's embassy in Washington, D.C., or the nearest consulate office.

## TIPPING NORMS

**Restaurants:** Tipping in restaurants is customary in the United States. It is standard to leave a gratuity of 20-25% of the total bill, depending on the quality of service. Some restaurants may automatically add a service charge for larger groups.

**Cafes and Bars**: Like restaurants, tipping between 20-25% for good service is expected in cafes and bars. If you order at the counter in a cafe, a small tip may be left in a designated jar.

**Hotels:** Hotel staff, including housekeeping and bellhops, appreciate tips for their services. A tip of $2-$5 per night for housekeeping and $1-$2 per bag for bellhops is customary.

**Transportation:** If using taxis or rideshare services, rounding up the fare or adding a 15-20% tip is customary. If a driver provides exceptional service or assistance, consider a higher tip.

Understanding and respecting these practical aspects will enhance your experience in Santa Fe, ensuring a smooth and enjoyable visit to the City Different.

# WEATHER AND CLIMATE

SPRING (MARCH TO MAY)

**Weather:** Spring in Santa Fe brings mild temperatures with daytime highs ranging from 50°F to 70°F. Evenings can be cool, averaging around 30°F to 40°F.

**What to Pack:**

1. Layers: Bring light jackets, sweaters, and long sleeves for cooler evenings.
2. Comfortable shoes: Ideal for exploring outdoor attractions and walking around the Plaza.
3. Umbrella: While spring is generally dry, occasional showers may occur.

## SUMMER (JUNE TO AUGUST)

**Weather:** Santa Fe experiences warm summers with daytime temperatures ranging from 80°F to 90°F. Nights are cooler, averaging around 50°F to 60°F.

**What to Pack:**

1. Light and breathable clothing: Shorts, t-shirts, and sundresses for daytime activities.
2. Sun protection: Sunscreen, sunglasses, and a wide-brimmed hat for sun-filled days.
3. Water bottle: Stay hydrated, especially when exploring outdoor attractions.

## FALL (SEPTEMBER TO NOVEMBER)

**Weather:** Fall brings cooler temperatures, with daytime highs ranging from 60°F to 70°F. Evenings can be chilly, averaging around 30°F to 40°F.

**What to Pack:**

1. Layers: Bring a mix of sweaters, jackets, and long sleeves for varying temperatures.
2. Comfortable walking shoes: Ideal for exploring outdoor events and fall festivals.
3. Camera: Capture the vibrant fall foliage in the surrounding landscapes.

## WINTER (DECEMBER TO FEBRUARY)

**Weather:** Winters in Santa Fe are cold, with daytime highs ranging from 30°F to 50°F. Nights can be frigid, averaging around 10°F to 20°F.

**What to Pack:**

1. Warm layers: Pack a heavy coat, thermal layers, gloves, and a hat for cold days and nights.
2. Winter boots are suitable for snowy or icy conditions, especially when planning outdoor activities.
3. Indoor activities: Bring books, tablets, or other indoor entertainment options for colder days.

## GENERAL PACKING TIPS

1. Comfortable Walking Shoes: Santa Fe is a walkable city with uneven terrain, so comfortable shoes are essential for exploring.
2. Sun Protection: The high-altitude desert sun can be intense, so pack sunscreen, sunglasses, and a hat.
3. Reusable Water Bottle: Stay hydrated, especially in the dry climate. Carry a reusable water bottle during outdoor activities.
4. Camera or Smartphone: Capture the beauty of Santa Fe's landscapes, architecture, and vibrant culture.

## SPECIAL EVENTS

1. **Festive Attire:** If visiting during events like Santa Fe Fiesta or holiday celebrations, consider packing festive attire for special occasions.
2. **Cultural Attire:** During events with Native American influences, wearing respectful and culturally appropriate attire is encouraged.

Understanding Santa Fe's seasonal weather variations and packing accordingly ensures a comfortable and enjoyable visit. Whether strolling through the Plaza in spring or exploring winter festivities, adapting your wardrobe to the season enhances your overall experience in the City Different.

# GETTING THERE AND AROUND

## TRANSPORTATION OPTIONS

### FLIGHTS: SANTA FE REGIONAL AIRPORT (SAF)

While Santa Fe has a regional airport, it primarily serves domestic flights. Many travelers opt to fly into Albuquerque International Sunport (ABQ), which is approximately an hour's drive from Santa Fe. Airlines like American, Delta, and Southwest operate regular flights to and from these airports.

### TRAINS: RAIL RUNNER EXPRESS

Connect with Santa Fe via the Rail Runner Express, a commuter train between Santa Fe and Albuquerque. The

Santa Fe Depot is conveniently located in the heart of downtown, providing easy access to the city.

## BUSES

**Greyhound:** Greyhound offers bus services connecting Santa Fe to various regional cities.

**Santa Fe Trails:** The local bus service, Santa Fe Trails, provides transportation within the city, making it easy to navigate critical areas.

## CARS

Driving from Albuquerque: Renting a car provides flexibility if arriving at Albuquerque International Sunport. Interstate 25 connects Albuquerque to Santa Fe, and the drive takes approximately one hour. Car rental companies are available at the airport.

## LOCAL PUBLIC TRANSPORTATION DETAILS

## SANTA FE TRAILS

Santa Fe Trails is the local bus service that operates throughout the city. It covers critical neighborhoods, attractions, and the downtown area. Check schedules and routes for convenient and cost-effective transportation.

## BIKING AND WALKING

Santa Fe is a pedestrian-friendly city with bike-friendly pathways. Many attractions and neighborhoods are easily explored on foot or by bicycle. Biking rental services are available for those exploring the city's charming streets and trails.

## DRIVING RULES AND RENTAL INFORMATION

### DRIVING RULES

1. In Santa Fe, as in the rest of the United States, driving is on the right side of the road.
2. Seat belts are mandatory for all passengers.
3. Follow speed limits, typically posted in miles per hour (mph).
4. Avoid using a mobile phone while driving unless it is hands-free.

### RENTAL INFORMATION

1. Major car rental companies operate at the Santa Fe Regional Airport and Albuquerque International Sunport. It is advisable to book in advance, especially during peak travel seasons.

2. Rental agencies may have different age restrictions and requirements, so check the terms and conditions before booking.

## AIRPORT AND MAJOR STATION INFORMATION

### SANTA FE REGIONAL AIRPORT (SAF)

1. It is located approximately 10 miles southwest of downtown Santa Fe.
2. It offers limited commercial flights and is often used for general aviation.
3. Ground transportation options include taxis and rental cars.

### ALBUQUERQUE INTERNATIONAL SUNPORT (ABQ)

1. The region's primary airport is about 60 miles south of Santa Fe.
2. Major airlines operate domestic and some international flights.
3. Ground transportation options include shuttles, taxis, and rental cars.

## SANTA FE DEPOT (TRAIN STATION)

1. The train station is located in downtown Santa Fe and is a Rail Runner Express hub.
2. The station is within walking distance of the Plaza and other downtown attractions.
3. Taxis and rideshare services are readily available for onward transportation.

Various transportation options make Navigating Santa Fe convenient, each offering a unique perspective on the city's beauty and charm. Whether by air, rail, bus, or car, visitors have the flexibility to tailor their journey and explore the diverse landscapes and cultural gems that Santa Fe has to offer.

# ACCOMMODATIONS

LUXURY HOTELS: PRICE RANGE: $300 - $800 PER NIGHT

**Rosewood Inn of the Anasazi: 113 Washington Ave, Santa Fe, NM 87501**

Nestled in the heart of Santa Fe's Historic District, the Rosewood Inn of the Anasazi is a boutique luxury hotel. It combines Southwestern charm with modern sophistication, offering beautifully appointed rooms, a fine dining restaurant, and a serene atmosphere.

**La Posada de Santa Fe, a Tribute Portfolio Resort & Spa: 330 E Palace Ave, Santa Fe, NM 87501**

This historic resort and spa showcases Santa Fe's rich cultural heritage. With adobe-style architecture and lush gardens, La Posada de Santa Fe offers luxury accommodations, a world-class spa, and a range of upscale dining options.

**Four Seasons Resort Rancho Encantado Santa Fe: 198 State Road 592, Santa Fe, NM 87506**

The Four Seasons Resort Rancho Encantado is just outside Santa Fe and offers a secluded and luxurious retreat. Surrounded by the breathtaking landscapes of the Sangre de Cristo Mountains, it features well-appointed casitas, a spa, and fine dining with panoramic views.

**Inn and Spa at Loretto: 211 Old Santa Fe Trail, Santa Fe, NM 87501**

Inspired by the traditional Taos Pueblo architecture, the Inn and Spa at Loretto is a luxury hotel near the Historic Plaza. It boasts a full-service spa, upscale accommodations, and the award-winning Luminaria Restaurant and Patio.

**Bishop's Lodge, Auberge Resorts Collection: 1297 Bishop's Lodge Rd, Santa Fe, NM 87501**

Nestled in a stunning natural setting, Bishop's Lodge offers a luxurious retreat with modern comfort and historic charm. Guests can enjoy spacious accommodations, outdoor activities, a spa, and gourmet dining.

## BOUTIQUE HOTELS: PRICE RANGE: $200 - $400 PER NIGHT

**Inn of the Five Graces: 150 E DeVargas St, Santa Fe, NM 87501**

This luxurious boutique inn features opulent Southwestern and Asian-inspired decor. The Inn of the Five Graces offers beautifully decorated rooms, lush gardens, and a serene atmosphere within walking distance of the Historic Plaza.

**El Rey Court: 1862 Cerrillos Rd, Santa Fe, NM 87505**

A mid-century modern gem, El Rey Court combines retro aesthetics with modern comfort. This boutique hotel features stylish rooms, a courtyard with a pool, and a vibrant atmosphere.

**Old Santa Fe Inn: 320 Galisteo St, Santa Fe, NM 87501**

The Old Santa Fe Inn offers a charming and intimate experience in the heart of downtown Santa Fe. The boutique hotel features cozy rooms, Southwestern decor, and a complimentary wine and cheese hour for guests.

**Hotel Santa Fe: 1501 Paseo De Peralta, Santa Fe, NM 87501**

Embracing the Native American Pueblo heritage, Hotel Santa Fe is a boutique hotel known for its warm hospitality. The hotel features traditional adobe-style architecture, handmade furnishings, and a solid commitment to sustainability.

**La Fonda on the Plaza: 100 E San Francisco St, Santa Fe, NM 87501**

With a history dating back to 1922, La Fonda on the Plaza is a boutique hotel located on the Historic Plaza. It blends Old World charm with modern amenities, offering unique rooms, a rooftop terrace, and the renowned La Plazuela restaurant.

## MID-RANGE OPTIONS: PRICE RANGE: $150 - $250 PER NIGHT

**La Quinta Inn by Wyndham Santa Fe: 4298 Cerrillos Rd, Santa Fe, NM 87507**

La Quinta Inn provides a convenient location with easy access to downtown Santa Fe. This mid-range hotel offers comfortable rooms, an outdoor pool, and complimentary breakfast.

**Drury Plaza Hotel in Santa Fe: 828 Paseo De Peralta, Santa Fe, NM 87501**

Located near the Historic Plaza, Drury Plaza Hotel offers a blend of historic charm and modern amenities. Guests can enjoy spacious rooms, an indoor/outdoor rooftop pool, and complimentary evening snacks and drinks.

**Courtyard by Marriott Santa Fe: 3347 Cerrillos Rd, Santa Fe, NM 87507**

Courtyard by Marriott provides a contemporary and comfortable stay. The hotel is close to shopping and dining, offering well-appointed rooms, a fitness center, and a restaurant serving breakfast and dinner.

**Inn of the Governors: 101 W Alameda St, Santa Fe, NM 87501**

Near the Historic Plaza, the Inn of the Governors is a mid-range hotel with a Southwestern ambiance. Guests can enjoy the lobby's cozy rooms, a heated outdoor pool, and complimentary tea and sherry.

**Hotel Chimayo de Santa Fe: 125 Washington Ave, Santa Fe, NM 87501**

Reflecting the rich cultural heritage of Chimayo, this hotel offers a unique and comfortable stay. Hotel Chimayo features vibrant rooms, a traditional courtyard, and a New Mexican cuisine restaurant.

## BUDGET-FRIENDLY CHOICES: PRICE RANGE: $80 - $150 PER NIGHT

**Santa Fe Sage Inn: 725 Cerrillos Rd, Santa Fe, NM 87505**

Santa Fe Sage Inn is a budget-friendly option with a modern Southwestern flair. It features comfortable rooms, an outdoor pool, and a complimentary shuttle service to the Historic Plaza.

**Motel 6 Santa Fe Central: 3470 Cerrillos Rd, Santa Fe, NM 87505**

Motel 6 offers straightforward and affordable accommodations. It is located near the Railyard Arts District and provides simple rooms, an outdoor pool, and pet-friendly options.

**Econo Lodge Inn & Suites: 3752 Cerrillos Rd, Santa Fe, NM 87507**

Econo Lodge Inn & Suites provides budget-friendly lodging with complimentary breakfast and Wi-Fi. It is conveniently situated for exploring attractions in and around Santa Fe.

**The Inn at Vanessie: 427 W Water St, Santa Fe, NM 87501**

The Inn at Vanessie offers budget-friendly accommodations with a unique charm. It provides simple yet comfortable rooms within walking distance of the Historic Plaza.

**Days Inn by Wyndham Santa Fe New Mexico: 2900 Cerrillos Rd, Santa Fe, NM 87507**

Days Inn is a budget-friendly option offering clean and comfortable rooms. It features amenities like an outdoor pool, complimentary breakfast, and easy access to major attractions.

# BUDGETING

## AVERAGE COSTS

### MEALS

1. **Budget:** $10 - $20 per meal at casual eateries, food trucks, and cafes.
2. **Mid-Range:** $20 - $50 per meal at mid-range restaurants and cafes.
3. **Fine Dining:** $50 and above per person for upscale dining experiences.

## TRANSPORTATION

1. **Public Transit:** Santa Fe Trails bus service costs $1 per ride, providing an affordable way to navigate the city.
2. **Rideshare/Taxis:** Short rides within the city typically range from $5 to $15.
3. **Car Rentals:** Rental car rates vary, starting at approximately $40 daily.

## ATTRACTIONS

1. **Museums and Galleries:** Admission fees range from $5 to $20, with some museums offering free or discounted entry on certain days.
2. **Historic Sites**: Entrance fees for historic sites like the Loretto Chapel or the San Miguel Mission can range from $2 to $10.
3. **Outdoor Activities:** Hiking or nature walks are generally free, but the costs of guided tours or equipment rentals may have additional fees.

## MONEY-SAVING TIPS

### DINING

1. **Explore Local Markets:** Visit the Santa Fe Farmers' Market or local food markets for affordable and fresh produce. Some markets offer prepared foods showcasing local flavors at reasonable prices.
2. **Happy Hour Specials:** Take advantage of happy hour specials at restaurants and bars for discounted drinks and appetizers. This is a great way to experience the culinary scene without breaking the bank.
3. **Picnics:** Enjoy the scenic beauty of Santa Fe by having a picnic in one of the city's parks or plazas. Purchase local ingredients and create your own affordable and enjoyable meal.

### TRANSPORTATION

1. **Use Public Transit:** Santa Fe Trails buses are an economical way to explore the city. Consider purchasing a day pass if you plan to use public transportation multiple times daily.
2. **Walking and Biking:** Many attractions are within walking or biking distance in Santa Fe. Take

advantage of the city's pedestrian-friendly layout to save on transportation costs.

3. **Carpool or Rideshare:** If traveling with others, consider carpooling or ridesharing to split transportation costs. This can be a cost-effective and environmentally friendly option.

## ATTRACTIONS

1. **Free Admission Days:** Take note of museums and attractions that offer free admission days or discounted rates during certain times. Plan your visits accordingly to maximize savings.
2. **City Passes:** Investigate if there are city passes or bundled tickets for multiple attractions. These passes often provide significant savings compared to purchasing individual tickets.
3. **Outdoor Activities:** Explore the natural beauty around Santa Fe by engaging in free or low-cost outdoor activities like hiking or nature walks. Many trails and scenic spots are accessible without an entrance fee.

## ACCOMMODATIONS

1. **Off-Peak Travel:** Consider visiting during off-peak seasons when accommodations may offer lower rates. This can also apply to flights and attractions.

2. **Book in Advance:** Secure accommodations and tickets in advance to take advantage of early booking discounts. This applies to hotels, tours, and some attractions.

3. **Consider Alternative Accommodations:** Explore options such as vacation rentals or guesthouses, which may offer competitive rates compared to traditional hotels.

Budgeting wisely in Santa Fe allows visitors to savor the city's unique offerings without straining their wallets. By taking advantage of local markets, happy hour specials, and budget-friendly transportation options, travelers can create memorable experiences while staying within their financial comfort zone.

# FUN FACTS AND TRIVIA

## HISTORICAL MILESTONES

**Oldest Capital City:** Santa Fe proudly holds the title of the oldest capital city in the United States, established in 1610 by Spanish colonists. Its rich history is woven into the very fabric of the town, with the Plaza at its core witnessing centuries of historical milestones.

**Santa Fe Trail:** The city played a crucial role in the 19th-century Santa Fe Trail, a trade route connecting Missouri with Santa Fe. This trail was instrumental in shaping the region's cultural exchange and economic development.

**Pueblo Revolt of 1680:** Santa Fe experienced a significant historical event when the Indigenous Pueblo people successfully staged a revolt against Spanish rule in 1680, leading to a temporary departure of Spanish settlers from the area.

## CULTURAL QUIRKS

**City Different:** Santa Fe's moniker, "The City Different," is not just a catchy phrase. It reflects the city's commitment to maintaining its unique character and resisting the standardization seen in many urban centers.

**Blue Doors:** It is expected to see houses with blue doors in Santa Fe. The tradition is rooted in the belief that blue represents protection and wards off evil spirits.

**Adobe Ordinance:** Santa Fe has a strict building code known as the "Santa Fe Style," emphasizing using Adobe and other traditional materials in construction. This ordinance ensures the preservation of the city's distinctive architectural heritage.

## NOTABLE LANDMARKS

**Palace of the Governors:** Built in 1610, the Palace of the Governors is the oldest continuously used public building in the U.S. It has served as a seat of government, military fortress, and trading post over the centuries.

**Loretto Chapel's Miraculous Staircase:** The Loretto Chapel is renowned for its "Miraculous Staircase," an architectural marvel with two complete 360-degree turns, built without a central support. The mystery surrounding its construction adds to its allure. The Loretto Chapel also holds an extraordinary place in the author's heart, as it was where Greg and I said our vows. It made for a very magical experience!

**Georgia O'Keeffe Museum:** Dedicated to the iconic American artist who found inspiration in the landscapes of New Mexico, this museum houses the most extensive collection of O'Keeffe's work, providing insight into her profound connection with the region.

Santa Fe's fun facts and trivia weave a tapestry of historical richness, cultural uniqueness, and architectural marvels, inviting visitors to delve into the layers of its fascinating narrative.

# EXPLORING NEIGHBORHOODS

## HISTORIC PLAZA DISTRICT

**Historic Plaza District: Timeless Charm and Tradition:** The Historic Plaza District exudes a timeless charm with its centuries-old architecture and cultural landmarks. Its central location makes it a bustling center of activity where tradition meets contemporary life. The Plaza is the epicenter of cultural events, Native American festivities, and an ever-present connection to Santa Fe's storied past.

**Santa Fe Plaza:** The heart and soul of Santa Fe, the Historic Plaza District, is a captivating blend of history, culture, and commerce. The Plaza, surrounded by adobe structures, has been a focal point since the city's establishment in 1610. Today, it serves as a vibrant gathering place, hosting events, markets, and celebrations. Explore the Palace of the

Governors, the oldest continuously used public building in the U.S., where Native American artisans display their crafts. The Plaza is also home to many shops, restaurants, and galleries, making it an ideal starting point for your Santa Fe journey.

**Cathedral Basilica of St. Francis of Assisi:** Adjacent to the Plaza, the Cathedral Basilica stands as a beacon of faith and architectural splendor. With its Romanesque Revival style and stunning stained-glass windows, the cathedral is a serene retreat offering a glimpse into Santa Fe's religious and artistic heritage.

RAILYARD ARTS DISTRICT

**Railyard Arts District: Fusion of History and Modernity:** The Railyard Arts District represents a harmonious blend of historical roots and modern innovation. It is a space where the echoes of the past merge with the vibrant pulse of contemporary art and culture. The district's adaptive reuse of the historic train depot and warehouses underscores Santa Fe's commitment to preserving its heritage while fostering a dynamic creative scene.

**Santa Fe Railyard:** A hub of creativity and innovation, the Railyard Arts District is a dynamic neighborhood that blends history with contemporary flair. Formerly a bustling train depot, the Railyard has become a cultural epicenter. Explore SITE Santa Fe, a cutting-edge modern art space, or wander through the vibrant galleries and studios showcasing diverse artistic expressions. The Railyard hosts the Santa Fe Farmers' Market, where local farmers and artisans converge to offer fresh produce, crafts, and a taste of the region's agricultural richness.

**Rail Runner Express Train Depot:** Embrace the district's historic roots at the Rail Runner Express Train Depot. This transportation hub connects Santa Fe to neighboring cities, allowing one to explore the region beyond the city limits. The depot's architecture reflects the city's commitment to preserving its rich history.

## CANYON ROAD ART GALLERIES

**Canyon Road: Artistic Extravaganza in Nature's Embrace:** Canyon Road stands as an artistic extravaganza framed by the natural beauty of Santa Fe. The street is a canvas adorned with galleries that spill over with color and creativity. Lush gardens and towering trees add to the ambiance, creating an immersive experience where art and nature intertwine.

**Canyon Road:** Renowned as an art lover's paradise, Canyon Road is a winding thoroughfare with over a hundred galleries, studios, and boutiques. Stroll through this picturesque street shaded by ancient trees and adobe walls adorned with vibrant flowers. The galleries showcase various artistic styles, from traditional Southwestern to contemporary and international works. Engage with artists in their studios and witness the creative energy that defines this enchanting arts district.

**Teatro Paraguas:** For a taste of performing arts, Teatro Paraguas on Canyon Road is a hidden gem. This intimate theater space presents a variety of performances, including plays, poetry readings, and live music. It is a cultural oasis where creativity flourishes, adding a dynamic layer to Canyon Road's artistic landscape.

Visitors explored these neighborhoods through Santa Fe's diverse facets, each offering a unique perspective on the city's rich tapestry. Whether wandering the historic Plaza, immersing in the creativity of the Railyard, or discovering the artistic treasures of Canyon Road, each neighborhood contributes to the City Different's multifaceted allure.

# LOCAL'S INSIGHT

## HIDDEN GEMS KNOWN TO LOCALS

**Ten Thousand Waves:** While renowned as a top-notch spa, locals cherish Ten Thousand Waves for its authentic Japanese-style hot tubs nestled in the mountains. The serene setting and communal tubs provide a unique relaxation experience.

**The Shed's Blue Corn Enchiladas:** Locals swear by The Shed, a historic restaurant in the heart of downtown Santa Fe, for serving the best blue corn enchiladas. This delectable dish showcases the region's culinary prowess.

**Randall Davey Audubon Center:** A hidden oasis for birdwatching and nature walks, this Audubon Center is a local gem offering tranquility just minutes from the city center. It is a haven for those seeking a peaceful escape.

**Rooftop Pools at La Fonda:** Locals often escape to the rooftop pools at La Fonda on the Plaza for a refreshing dip with panoramic city views. It is a secret retreat, providing a unique perspective of Santa Fe.

## CULTURAL ETIQUETTE AND CUSTOMS

**Respect for Pueblo Traditions:** Santa Fe has strong ties to nearby Pueblos, and locals emphasize respecting their traditions. If attending a Pueblo event or ceremony, it is customary to ask permission before taking photos and to be mindful of cultural sensitivities.

**Appreciation for Art:** With a city so deeply rooted in the arts, locals appreciate genuine interest and respect for the numerous galleries and studios. It is common to start conversations with artists, often in their galleries.

**Slow Pace of Life:** Santa Feans embrace a slower pace of life. Visitors are encouraged to stroll through the Plaza, linger in cafes, and savor the moment. Rushing is contrary to the city's laid-back ethos.

**Diverse Cuisine Etiquette:** Santa Fe's culinary scene reflects various flavors. Locals appreciate adventurous palates and willingness to try Southwestern and Native American-inspired dishes. Dining etiquette includes savoring each bite and enjoying the regional ingredients.

## BEST TIMES TO VISIT FOR AUTHENTIC EXPERIENCES

**Santa Fe Indian Market (August):** This annual event showcases the work of Native American artists and craftspeople. Locals recommend attending to witness the vibrant art scene and engage with artists.

**Fiesta de Santa Fe (September):** Celebrating the city's history, Fiesta de Santa Fe is a time-honored tradition. Locals advise visiting during this festival to taste Santa Fe's rich cultural heritage through parades, music, and dance.

**Off-Season Exploration (Winter):** While summer is popular, locals find the winter season enchanting. The city is adorned with holiday lights, and the crisp air creates a cozy atmosphere. It is an ideal time for exploring without the crowds.

**Spring Arts Festival (April):** Santa Fe blooms with artistic expression during the Spring Arts Festival. Locals suggest visiting in April to witness the city coming alive with gallery openings, art markets, and outdoor performances.

By embracing these local insights, visitors can delve beyond the surface of Santa Fe, experiencing the city as the locals do

—immersing themselves in hidden gems, respecting cultural nuances, and timing their visit for an authentic, enriching experience.

# CULINARY DELIGHTS

## ICONIC SOUTHWESTERN DISHES

**Green and Red Chile:** Santa Fe is synonymous with the unique and flavorful red and green chiles that define Southwestern cuisine. From breakfast burritos to enchiladas, locals infuse these chiles into myriad dishes, offering a spicy and aromatic culinary experience.

**Blue Corn Tamales:** Blue corn, indigenous to the region, finds its way into traditional dishes like tamales. These flavorful bundles, often stuffed with savory fillings, showcase the local emphasis on indigenous ingredients.

**Navajo Tacos:** A fusion of Native American and Hispanic influences, Navajo Tacos feature fry bread topped with seasoned meats, beans, cheese, and fresh vegetables. This satisfying dish is both delicious and culturally significant.

## MUST-TRY RESTAURANTS AND CAFES

**Tia Sophia's: 210 W San Francisco St, Santa Fe, NM 87501**

A Santa Fe institution, Tia Sophia's is a classic diner-style restaurant famous for its breakfast burritos smothered in red or green chile. It is a casual spot with a warm atmosphere, perfect for a hearty Southwestern meal.

**Café Pasqual's: 121 Don Gaspar Ave, Santa Fe, NM 87501**

A beloved establishment, Café Pasqual's is a culinary gem offering creative Southwestern-inspired dishes made with locally sourced, organic ingredients. Each dish is a culinary masterpiece, from huevos rancheros to green chile stew.

**The Shed: 113½ E Palace Ave, Santa Fe, NM 87501**

Nestled in the heart of the historic district, The Shed is an iconic restaurant serving Northern New Mexican cuisine. Locals and visitors flock to savor dishes like blue corn enchiladas and carne adovada in a charming adobe setting.

**Geronimo: 724 Canyon Rd, Santa Fe, NM 87501**

Upscale dining with a diverse menu, offering a blend of American, French, and Asian-inspired dishes.

**Sazón: 221 Shelby St, Santa Fe, NM 87501**

Known for its upscale take on Southwestern cuisine, Sazon offers a sophisticated dining experience. The menu showcases a fusion of flavors, featuring mole, posole, and ancho-chile-rubbed steaks.

I love Sazon so much, from their hospitality to their brigade style service, to their creative and fantastic cuisine, and the personal touch that James Beard Award Winning Chef Fernando Olea adds to everything that I had them host my wedding reception, which was nothing short of spectacular. You can not visit Santa Fe without treating yourself to a meal at this restaurant. But make sure to book a reservation. You will not regret it!

**Coyote Café: 132 W Water St, Santa Fe, NM 87501**

Contemporary American cuisine with a Southwestern twist is known for its creative and artful dishes.

**La Choza: 905 Alarid St, Santa Fe, NM 87505**

A sister restaurant to The Shed, La Choza serves traditional New Mexican dishes in a vibrant and casual setting.

**The Compound Restaurant: 653 Canyon Rd, Santa Fe, NM 87501**

Fine dining in a historic adobe building, serving a seasonal menu inspired by global and regional influences.

**Santa Fe Bite: 311 Old Santa Fe Trail, Santa Fe, NM 87501**

Known for its green chile cheeseburgers, Santa Fe Bite offers classic American comfort food.

**Tune-Up Café: 1115 Hickox St, Santa Fe, NM 87505**

A local favorite for breakfast, brunch, and lunch, featuring diverse dishes with a Southwestern twist.

**Jambo Café: 2010 Cerrillos Rd, Santa Fe, NM 87505**

An award-winning restaurant serving vibrant and flavorful African-Caribbean fusion cuisine.

**Anasazi Restaurant at Rosewood Inn: 113 Washington Ave, Santa Fe, NM 87501**

Contemporary American cuisine with a Southwestern flair is served in an elegant and historic setting.

**Paper Dosa: 551 W Cordova Rd, Santa Fe, NM 87505**

It is a popular spot for South Indian cuisine, offering dosas, curries, and other flavorful dishes.

**Clafoutis: 333 W Cordova Rd, Santa Fe, NM 87505**

A charming French bakery and café known for its pastries, quiches, and breakfast items.

**Maria's New Mexican Kitchen: 555 W Cordova Rd, Santa Fe, NM 87505**

A popular spot for traditional New Mexican dishes, known for its extensive margarita menu.

**The Pantry: 1820 Cerrillos Rd, Santa Fe, NM 87505**

A classic diner-style restaurant serving breakfast, brunch, and New Mexican comfort food.

**Shake Foundation: 631 Cerrillos Rd, Santa Fe, NM 87505**

A casual spot is known for its gourmet burgers, hot dogs, and hand-spun milkshakes.

**Il Piatto: 95 W Marcy St, Santa Fe, NM 87501**

An Italian trattoria offers handmade pasta, wood-fired pizzas, and a selection of Italian-inspired dishes.

**Counter Culture Café: 930 Baca St, Santa Fe, NM 87505**

A cozy café focusing on organic and locally sourced ingredients offers breakfast and lunch options.

**Second Street Brewery: Location: Multiple locations**

A local brewery with pub-style fare, including burgers, sandwiches, and various craft beers.

These restaurants and cafes in Santa Fe provide a diverse range of culinary experiences, from traditional New Mexican flavors to international and contemporary cuisine. Enjoy exploring the vibrant food scene in the City Different!

## CULINARY EVENTS AND FESTIVALS

**Santa Fe Farmers' Market:** Held year-round, the Santa Fe Farmers' Market is a vibrant showcase of local produce, artisanal products, and handmade crafts. Visitors can directly savor fresh fruits, vegetables, and unique Southwestern flavors from local farmers and vendors.

**Santa Fe Wine and Chile Fiesta:** This annual festival celebrates the region's dynamic culinary scene, pairing delectable dishes with wines from local vineyards. It is an opportunity to indulge in the rich flavors of Santa Fe's gastronomic offerings.

**Traditional Pueblo Feast Days:** Visitors can experience authentic Native American cuisine during classic Pueblo Feast Days. These events often include communal meals, dances, and cultural demonstrations, providing insight into the region's Indigenous food traditions.

Santa Fe's culinary landscape is a vibrant tapestry of Southwestern flavors, indigenous ingredients, and creative fusions. Whether savoring iconic dishes, dining in renowned restaurants, or immersing in culinary festivals, visitors are in for a gastronomic journey that captures the essence of this unique and flavorful city.

# FUN FOR ALL AGES

## TODDLER-FRIENDLY ACTIVITIES

**Santa Fe Children's Museum: 1050 Old Pecos Trail, Santa Fe, NM 87505**

Tailored for the youngest adventurers, the Children's Museum offers interactive exhibits, a miniature adobe village, and a captivating outdoor space. Toddlers can engage in imaginative play, explore sensory exhibits, and enjoy age-appropriate activities.

**Randall Davey Park: 1800 Upper Canyon Rd, Santa Fe, NM 87501**

Randall Davey Park is perfect for a family outing with gentle trails and open spaces. Toddlers can delight in the colorful flora, spot wildlife, and enjoy the fresh mountain air. The park provides a serene environment for toddlers to explore nature at their own pace.

## Meow Wolf's House of Eternal Return: 1352 Rufina Cir, Santa Fe, NM 87507

This immersive and interactive art experience captivates toddlers and parents alike. With surreal environments, secret passages, and whimsical exhibits, Meow Wolf stimulates young minds and sparks creativity.

## Railyard Park: 740 Cerrillos Rd, Santa Fe, NM 87505

Railyard Park offers a spacious and safe environment for toddlers to play. The park includes a playground with age-appropriate equipment, a splash pad for water play during the warmer months, and open spaces for picnics.

## Harrell House Bug Museum: 433 Paseo de Peralta, Santa Fe, NM 87501

Toddlers are often fascinated with bugs, making the Harrell House Bug Museum an exciting destination. The museum features live insects, educational exhibits, and interactive displays suitable for young children.

## Santa Fe Botanical Garden: 715 Camino Lejo, Santa Fe, NM 87505

The Santa Fe Botanical Garden provides a peaceful setting for toddlers and their families to explore nature. The Children's Play Area within the garden includes interactive elements, sensory gardens, and opportunities for imaginative play.

**El Rancho de las Golondrinas - Living History Museum: 334 Los Pinos Road, Santa Fe, NM 87507**

Toddlers can return in time at El Rancho de las Golondrinas, an outdoor living history museum. The site features historic buildings, farm animals, and demonstrations that offer young visitors a hands-on and immersive experience.

## TEENAGER EXCITEMENT: THRILLS AND ENTERTAINMENT

**Meow Wolf: 1352 Rufina Cir, Santa Fe, NM 87507**

Meow Wolf is an immersive and interactive art experience that appeals to teenagers' creativity and sense of adventure. The House of Eternal Return features mind-bending exhibits, secret passages, and a unique blend of art and technology.

**Santa Fe Climbing Center: 3008 Cielo Ct, Santa Fe, NM 87507**

For active teenagers, the Santa Fe Climbing Center offers indoor rock-climbing challenges suitable for all skill levels. It is a great way to engage in physical activity while having fun.

**Ghost Tour: Santa Fe Ghost and History Tours, various providers**

Santa Fe's rich history lends itself to intriguing ghost tours. Teenagers can enjoy a spooky and entertaining evening while learning about the city's historical and paranormal tales.

**Santa Fe Railyard Arts District: 740 Cerrillos Rd, Santa Fe, NM 87505**

The Railyard Arts District provides a vibrant atmosphere for teenagers to explore. It features art galleries, shops, and unique spaces, creating an urban and artsy experience.

**Santa Fe Mountain Adventures - Mountain Biking: Various trailheads around Santa Fe**

Rent bikes and explore trails like the Dale Ball or La Tierra Trails for a thrilling outdoor adventure. Santa Fe's extensive trail system offers compelling mountain biking opportunities. Teens can navigate the diverse terrain of La Tierra Trails, enjoying the adrenaline rush surrounded by breathtaking landscapes.

These teenager-friendly activities in Santa Fe combine art, adventure, and exploration, ensuring an enjoyable experience for older kids and teenagers.

## YOUNG ADULT ADVENTURES

**Santa Fe Railyard Arts District: 740 Cerrillos Rd, Santa Fe, NM 87505**

Young adults can explore the vibrant Railyard District, filled with contemporary art galleries, trendy boutiques, and hip cafes. It is a hub of creativity and a perfect spot for those seeking a modern and dynamic atmosphere.

**Sunset Hot Air Balloon Ride:**

Soar above the city in a hot air balloon for a breathtaking aerial perspective of Santa Fe. Young adults can enjoy the romance of a sunset ride, taking in panoramic views of the landscapes and the city's distinctive architecture.

**Georgia O'Keeffe's Ghost Ranch Tour: HC 77, Abiquiu, NM 87510 ·**

Delve into the artistic legacy of Georgia O'Keeffe with a tour of Ghost Ranch. Young adults can explore the landscapes that inspired the artist and gain insight into her creative process.

**Art Crawl on Canyon Road**

Canyon Road is renowned for its art galleries and studios. Young adults can spend an afternoon exploring this historic arts district, discovering contemporary and traditional artworks, and interacting with local artists.

**Santa Fe Brewing Company Tour: 35 Fire Pl, Santa Fe, NM 87508**

Santa Fe Brewing Company offers brewery tours for those interested in craft beer. Young adults can enjoy learning about brewing, tasting different beers, and experiencing the laid-back atmosphere.

**Santa Fe Farmers' Market: 1607 Paseo de Peralta, Santa Fe, NM 87501**

The Santa Fe Farmers' Market is a vibrant local produce, crafts, and food hub. Young adults can explore the market, try artisanal treats, and soak in the lively atmosphere.

**Santa Fe Hiking and Hot Springs:**

Embark on a day of adventure by hiking in the picturesque landscapes surrounding Santa Fe. After a rewarding hike, relax in a nearby natural hot springs, such as the Ten Thousand Waves spa, for a soothing and rejuvenating experience.

**Live Music at The Bridge at Santa Fe Brewing Company: 37 Fire Pl, Santa Fe, NM 87508**

Check out live music events at The Bridge, an outdoor venue at Santa Fe Brewing Company. It is a popular spot for concerts and gatherings.

**Santa Fe Street Food Institute: 418 Cerrillos Rd, Santa Fe, NM 87501**

Attend a cooking class or food event at the Santa Fe Street Food Institute. It is a hands-on experience for young adults interested in culinary adventures.

**Outdoor Yoga and Wellness Retreats:**

Participate in outdoor yoga sessions or wellness retreats in and around Santa Fe. It is a refreshing way for young adults to connect with nature and focus on well-being.

## ADULT AND SENIOR SERENITY: RELAXATION AND ENJOYMENT

**Santa Fe Botanical Garden: 715 Camino Lejo, Santa Fe, NM 87505**

Appreciate the tranquility of the Santa Fe Botanical Garden, featuring themed gardens and walking paths. It is an ideal setting for a stroll, surrounded by native plants and seasonal blooms.

**Santa Fe Opera: 301 Opera Dr, Santa Fe, NM 87506**

Experience cultural enrichment at the Santa Fe Opera. Seniors can enjoy world-class performances in a stunning outdoor amphitheater, combining the arts with the beauty of the New Mexico night sky.

## Ten Thousand Waves Spa: 21 Ten Thousand Waves Way, Santa Fe, NM 87501

For ultimate relaxation, seniors can indulge in the serenity of Ten Thousand Waves Spa. Nestled in the mountains, this Japanese-inspired spa offers therapeutic hot tubs and rejuvenating spa treatments in a peaceful setting.

## Georgia O'Keeffe Museum: 217 Johnson St, Santa Fe, NM 87501

Explore the art of Georgia O'Keeffe at this museum dedicated to the iconic American modernist painter. It offers a tranquil setting to appreciate her masterpieces.

## Loretto Chapel and Miraculous Staircase: 207 Old Santa Fe Trail, Santa Fe, NM 87501

Visit the historic Loretto Chapel and marvel at the Miraculous Staircase, an architectural wonder with a fascinating history.

## Santa Fe Plaza: Downtown Santa Fe

Stroll through the historic Santa Fe Plaza, surrounded by shops, galleries, and restaurants. It is a central hub for cultural events and gatherings.

## Santa Fe Margarita Trail

Explore the Santa Fe Margarita Trail, sampling signature margaritas at various restaurants and bars. It is a delightful way to experience the city's culinary scene.

**Historic Canyon Road Galleries**

Wander along Canyon Road, known for its art galleries and sculptures. It is a leisurely and cultural experience showcasing a variety of artistic expressions.

**Santa Fe Hiking Trails - Dale Ball Trails**

Take a scenic hike on the Dale Ball Trails, offering various routes with stunning views of the surrounding mountains and city.

**Santa Fe Culinary Classes**

Join a culinary class or food tour to explore the flavors of Santa Fe. It is a delightful way for adults and seniors to engage in hands-on culinary experiences.

Santa Fe caters to all age groups, ensuring diverse activities for toddlers, teenagers, adults, and seniors. Whether you are seeking family-friendly adventures, adrenaline-pumping thrills, cultural explorations, or serene relaxation, the city offers a well-rounded and inclusive experience for visitors of all ages.

# OUTDOOR ACTIVITIES

## HIKING TRAILS AND NATURE WALKS

**Dale Ball Trails:** Offering a network of interconnected trails just minutes from downtown, the Dale Ball Trails cater to hikers of all levels. The trails wind through the piñon and juniper-covered hills, providing panoramic views of the city and surrounding mountains. It is an ideal spot for a peaceful nature walk or an invigorating hike.

**Atalaya Mountain Trail:** The Atalaya Mountain Trail is popular for those seeking more challenges. The trailhead is located at St. John's College, and the hike takes you through fragrant ponderosa pine forests to the summit of Atalaya Mountain. The reward is a breathtaking panorama of the Sangre de Cristo Mountains and the city below.

**Bandelier National Monument:** A short drive from Santa Fe, Bandelier National Monument offers a fascinating blend of nature and history. Hike the Main Loop Trail to explore ancient cliff dwellings, petroglyphs, and the scenic Frijoles Canyon. It is a journey into the cultural and natural heritage of the region.

## ADRENALINE-PUMPING ADVENTURES

**White Water Rafting on the Rio Grande:** Experience the thrill of white water rafting on the Rio Grande. Several outfitters offer guided trips through the stunning canyons, providing an adrenaline-pumping adventure amidst the rapids and rugged landscapes.

**Ski Santa Fe:** In winter, Ski Santa Fe transforms into a haven for snow enthusiasts. Skiing and snowboarding enthusiasts can enjoy the crisp mountain air and stunning alpine scenery with various slopes catering to different skill levels.

**Mountain Biking in La Cuchara Trail:** La Cuchara Trail offers an exhilarating mountain biking experience. The trail, winding through the foothills, provides challenging terrain and rewarding views of the surrounding landscapes. It is a favorite among mountain biking enthusiasts looking for an adrenaline-fueled ride.

## SCENIC DRIVES AND DAY TRIPS

**High Road to Taos:** Embark on the High Road to Taos for a scenic drive through picturesque landscapes, charming villages, and historic churches. The route takes you through the Sangre de Cristo Mountains, offering breathtaking vistas and a glimpse into Northern New Mexico's cultural heritage.

**Abiquiú and Ghost Ranch:** Take a day trip to Abiquiú and Ghost Ranch, made famous by the artist Georgia O'Keeffe. Explore the stunning landscapes that inspired her iconic paintings, including the red rock formations and vibrant desert scenery.

**Turquoise Trail:** A historic route connecting Santa Fe to Albuquerque, the Turquoise Trail is a scenic drive through the Ortiz Mountains. Along the way, discover the artistic community of Madrid, visit the ghost town of Golden, and immerse yourself in the region's mining history.

Santa Fe's outdoor activities cater to nature lovers, thrill-seekers, and those seeking the tranquility of the great outdoors. Whether hiking amid the piñon trees, conquering challenging mountain biking trails, or embarking on scenic drives through the high desert, visitors are bound to discover the diverse and captivating landscapes surrounding the City Different.

# INDOOR ACTIVITIES

## MUSEUMS AND ART GALLERIES

**Georgia O'Keeffe Museum:** Immerse yourself in the artistry of one of America's most iconic painters, Georgia O'Keeffe. The museum houses a vast collection of her works, providing insight into her profound connection with the landscapes of New Mexico. It is a must-visit for art enthusiasts and those curious about the intersection of nature and art.

**Museum of International Folk Art:** Step into a world of vibrant colors and cultural diversity at the Museum of International Folk Art. Featuring a vast collection of folk art from around the globe, the museum showcases the creativity and craftsmanship of artists from diverse cultures—

intricately crafted textiles, ceramics, and traditional artifacts transport visitors to different corners of the world.

**SITE Santa Fe:** As a contemporary art space, SITE Santa Fe pushes the boundaries of artistic expression. The ever-changing exhibits highlight cutting-edge works from local and international artists, offering visitors a dynamic and thought-provoking experience.

## COZY CAFES AND BOOKSTORES

**Iconik Coffee Roasters:** Unwind in the inviting atmosphere of Iconik Coffee Roasters, a local favorite. Known for its specialty coffee blends and artisanal pastries, it is an ideal spot to relax, savor a cup of meticulously brewed coffee, and perhaps engage in people-watching.

**Op.Cit Books:** Explore the shelves of Op.Cit Books is a charming independent bookstore nestled in the heart of downtown Santa Fe. With its cozy ambiance and a curated selection of books, including regional titles and rare finds, it is a haven for book lovers seeking literary treasures.

**Teahouse Santa Fe:** For a tranquil escape, visit the Teahouse Santa Fe. This teahouse boasts an extensive tea menu from around the world, paired with a cozy ambiance. Whether you are a tea connoisseur or seeking a peaceful retreat, this spot offers a unique blend of relaxation and cultural exploration.

## PERFORMING ARTS VENUES

**The Lensic Performing Arts Center:** Immerse yourself in the world of performing arts at The Lensic, a historic venue that hosts various events, including concerts, theater productions, and dance performances. The beautifully restored theater provides an elegant setting for enjoying the cultural richness of Santa Fe.

**Santa Fe Opera House:** Experience the magic of opera in the breathtaking setting of the Santa Fe Opera House. Nestled in the hills, this open-air venue offers world-class productions against the backdrop of the New Mexico sunset, creating a truly enchanting experience for performing arts enthusiasts.

**Santa Fe Playhouse:** For a more intimate theater experience, the Santa Fe Playhouse, one of the oldest continuously operating community theaters in the country, presents a diverse range of theatrical performances. The Playhouse contributes to Santa Fe's vibrant arts scene, from classic plays to contemporary works.

Santa Fe's indoor activities invite visitors to explore the city's artistic soul and cultural heritage. Whether wandering through world-class museums, sipping tea in a cozy cafe, or attending a captivating performance, the City Different offers a rich tapestry of indoor experiences for every taste and inclination.

# ACTIVITIES FOR ALL SEASONS

## WINTER WONDERLAND: SKIING AND FESTIVALS

**Ski Santa Fe:** Embrace the winter wonderland of Santa Fe with a visit to Ski Santa Fe, a premier ski destination just a short drive from the city. Nestled in the Sangre de Cristo Mountains, the resort offers skiers and snowboarders a diverse range of slopes catering to various skill levels. With crisp mountain air and stunning alpine scenery, it is a winter paradise for outdoor enthusiasts.

**Farolito Walk on Canyon Road:** Experience the magic of Santa Fe's winter nights during the annual Farolito Walk on Canyon Road. Luminarias (small, candle-lit lanterns) line the historic street, creating a warm and enchanting atmosphere. Galleries stay open late, and the air is filled with the sounds of carolers, making it a festive and memorable holiday tradition.

**Santa Fe Winter Indian Market:** Held in December, the Winter Indian Market is a unique celebration of Native American art and culture. Artists from various tribes gather to showcase their work, allowing visitors to purchase one-of-a-kind handmade crafts, jewelry, and traditional artworks.

## SPRING BLOOMS: GARDENS AND CULTURAL EVENTS

**Santa Fe Botanical Garden:** As spring unfolds, the Santa Fe Botanical Garden bursts into vibrant blooms. Stroll through themed gardens, such as the Ojos y Manos Garden, showcasing native plants, or the Orchard Gardens with fruit trees in bloom. It is a tranquil oasis where the colors of spring come to life.

**Santa Fe Renaissance Fair:** Transport yourself back in time at the Santa Fe Renaissance Fair, typically held in spring. This lively event features period costumes, jousting tournaments, and artisanal crafts, creating a whimsical atmosphere that delights visitors of all ages.

**Santa Fe International Folk Art Market:** Celebrate global diversity at the Santa Fe International Folk Art Market in July. This event brings together master artists from around the world, showcasing traditional crafts, textiles, and artworks. It is an opportunity to immerse yourself in the rich cultural heritage of diverse communities.

## SUMMER ESCAPES: OUTDOOR CONCERTS AND FESTIVITIES

**Santa Fe Bandstand:** Enjoy the warm summer evenings with live music at Santa Fe Bandstand, a series of outdoor concerts in the historic downtown Plaza. From jazz to rock, the diverse lineup caters to various musical tastes, creating a vibrant and communal atmosphere under the starlit sky.

**Santa Fe Opera Tailgate Parties:** Enhance your opera experience with a tailgate party at the Santa Fe Opera. Before the performance begins, patrons gather in the parking lot for picnics, creating a festive atmosphere. It is a unique and social way to enjoy world-class opera against the backdrop of the New Mexico landscape.

**Spanish Market:** Immerse yourself in the rich Hispanic culture of Santa Fe at the annual Spanish Market in July. Artists showcase traditional Spanish Colonial art, including woodcarvings, tinwork, and handwoven textiles. The event also features live music, dance performances, and delicious Spanish cuisine.

## FALL FOLIAGE: HARVEST CELEBRATIONS AND ART WALKS

**Santa Fe Wine Harvest Festival:** As autumn colors paint the landscapes, indulge in the season's flavors at the Santa Fe Wine Harvest Festival. Held at the Santa Fe Opera, this event features wine tastings, live music, and culinary delights, celebrating the grape harvest in a picturesque setting.

**Aspens in the Sangre de Cristo Mountains:** Take a scenic drive to the Sangre de Cristo Mountains in the fall, where the aspen trees create a golden canopy. Hiking trails, such as the Aspen Vista Trail, offer breathtaking views of the vibrant foliage, making it a favorite destination for leaf-peeping enthusiasts.

**Santa Fe Art Walks:** Explore the city's artistic neighborhoods during fall art walks, such as those in the Railyard Arts District. Galleries stay open late, allowing visitors to appreciate the autumn ambiance while discovering new works by local and international artists.

Santa Fe's activities for all seasons showcase the city's versatility and the diverse experiences it offers year-round. Whether skiing in winter, strolling through blooming gardens in spring, attending outdoor concerts in summer, or celebrating the fall harvest, each season in Santa Fe brings unique charm and engaging activities for all to enjoy.

# TOP 10 LISTS

## TOP 10 HIDDEN GEMS

**Kakawa Chocolate House:** Tucked away from the main tourist thoroughfares, Kakawa Chocolate House is a delightful hidden gem. This artisanal chocolate shop offers an array of historic drinking chocolates and truffles. The cozy ambiance and unique flavors make it a sweet escape for those in the know.

**El Rancho de las Golondrinas:** A living history museum that often goes under the radar, El Rancho de las Golondrinas provides a glimpse into colonial New Mexico. The meticulously preserved buildings and engaging demonstrations offer a serene retreat into the region's past.

**Meow Wolf's House of Eternal Return:** While gaining popularity, Meow Wolf's immersive art installation remains a hidden gem for many. This surreal and interactive experience takes visitors through fantastical realms, challenging perceptions and sparking creativity.

**Cerrillos Hills State Park:** Just a short drive from Santa Fe, Cerrillos Hills State Park offers serene hiking trails and panoramic views. The historic mining town of Cerrillos adds a touch of authenticity, making it a hidden oasis for nature enthusiasts.

**El Santuario de Chimayó:** A spiritual and cultural gem, this is a pilgrimage site with a rich history. The small chapel, known for its miraculous dirt, welcomes visitors seeking a contemplative experience.

**Santuario de Guadalupe:** Nestled in the heart of downtown Santa Fe, Santuario de Guadalupe is a hidden architectural gem. With its distinctive blue dome, this historic church offers a tranquil space for reflecting and appreciating religious art.

**Canyon Road Sculpture Garden:** Adjacent to the more famous Canyon Road art galleries, the Sculpture Garden is often overlooked. It features outdoor sculptures by local and international artists, providing a serene and contemplative space amidst the creative energy of Canyon Road.

**LewAllen Galleries:** A hidden gem for art connoisseurs, LewAllen Galleries showcases contemporary and modern art. The expansive space features works by established and emerging artists.

**Gig Performance Space:** For those seeking intimate live music experiences, Gig Performance Space is a hidden gem. This cozy venue hosts a variety of musical performances, from jazz and folk to indie, providing a unique and eclectic atmosphere.

**Dixon's Farmers' Market:** A hidden treasure for food enthusiasts, the Dixon's Farmers' Market is held in the charming village of Dixon. Local vendors offer fresh produce, handmade crafts, and a taste of the region's agricultural bounty.

## TOP 10 TOURIST TRAPS TO AVOID

**Old Town Plaza Shops:** The shops around Old Town Plaza can be tourist traps, with inflated prices for souvenirs. Exploring alternative shopping districts might provide more authentic items for less.

**Horse-Drawn Carriage Rides:** While picturesque, horse-drawn carriage rides in the Plaza area can be considered tourist traps due to their high prices. Exploring the city on foot or with more affordable transportation options is recommended.

**Crystal Shops on Canyon Road:** Some crystal shops can be tourist traps with overpriced items. Visitors interested in crystals might find better value at alternative shops in different areas.

**Oldest House:** The "Oldest House" can be a tourist trap, as the title is debated among historic homes in the city. Visitors interested in history may enjoy more verified historical sites.

**Santa Fe Trolley Tours:** While convenient, trolley tours can be tourist traps with limited flexibility and high prices. Exploring the city at your own pace or joining smaller, more personalized tours might offer a more enjoyable experience.

**Plaza Street Performers:** While entertaining, some street performers around the Plaza can be seen as tourist traps with pressure for tips. Enjoying local talent at alternative venues may provide a more authentic experience.

**Indian Market Mass-Produced Crafts:** During the Indian Market, some vendors sell mass-produced crafts that can be considered tourist traps. Seek authentic, handmade items from reputable artists to support the local Native American community.

**Overpriced Art on Canyon Road:** Some galleries may overprice their art for the tourist market. Exploring alternative art districts or negotiating prices directly with artists may offer a more satisfying art-buying experience.

**Santa Fe Ghost Tours:** While entertaining, some ghost tours can be tourist traps with exaggerated stories and high prices. Exploring the city's haunted history through self-guided tours or reputable guides may provide a more authentic experience.

**Restaurants in Tourist Areas**: Restaurants located in heavily touristy areas like the Plaza may charge higher prices for food and drinks than establishments in less touristy parts of the city.

Navigating Santa Fe with an awareness of its hidden gems and potential tourist traps allows visitors to craft a personalized and authentic experience in the City Different. By exploring beyond the well-trodden paths and being discerning about attractions, travelers can uncover the true essence of this unique and culturally rich destination.

# EVENTS AND FESTIVALS

**Santa Fe Restaurant Week (February):** Kick off the year with a culinary adventure during Santa Fe Restaurant Week. Local restaurants offer prix-fixe menus, allowing diners to savor various dishes and flavors at exceptional prices. It is a fantastic opportunity to explore the city's vibrant culinary scene.

**Santa Fe Film Festival (February/March):** Celebrate the art of filmmaking at the Santa Fe Film Festival. Showcasing a diverse selection of independent and international films, the festival attracts filmmakers, industry professionals, and cinephiles alike. Screenings, panel discussions, and special events contribute to the vibrant film culture of Santa Fe.

**Santa Fe Bandstand (Summer):** Enjoy the rhythm of summer at Santa Fe Bandstand, a series of free outdoor concerts held in the historic downtown Plaza. From jazz and blues to rock and world music, the diverse lineup attracts locals and visitors, creating a lively and communal atmosphere.

**Santa Fe International Folk Art Market (July):** Immerse yourself in global craftsmanship at the Santa Fe International Folk Art Market. Artists from around the world gather to showcase traditional crafts, textiles, and artworks. The market provides a unique opportunity to connect with diverse cultures and support artisans.

**Santa Fe Indian Market (August):** One of the largest and most renowned Native American art markets in the world, the Santa Fe Indian Market transforms the city into a cultural hub. Native American artists from various tribes gather to showcase their extraordinary craftsmanship, from traditional jewelry and textiles to contemporary and innovative works.

**Santa Fe Fiesta (September):** Embrace the city's rich Hispanic heritage during Santa Fe Fiesta. This annual celebration commemorates the Spanish resettlement of Santa Fe in 1712. Festivities include a historical reenactment, processions, live music, and traditional dances, creating a lively and colorful atmosphere.

**Santa Fe Wine and Chile Fiesta (September):** Indulge in the rich flavors of the region at the Santa Fe Wine and Chile Fiesta. This culinary extravaganza brings together renowned chefs and winemakers for tastings, wine seminars, and gourmet events. It is a celebration of the vibrant culinary scene that defines Santa Fe.

**Santa Fe Independent Film Festival (October):** The Santa Fe Independent Film Festival is a must-attend event for cinephiles. Showcasing a diverse selection of independent films, this festival highlights emerging filmmakers and fosters a vibrant film community in the city.

**International Balloon Fiesta (October):** While not in Santa Fe proper, the nearby Albuquerque International Balloon Fiesta is a must-see event. Experience the mesmerizing sight of hundreds of hot air balloons filling the sky with vibrant colors. The event features mass ascensions, night glows, and a festive atmosphere.

**Farolito Walk on Canyon Road (December):** Welcome the holiday season with the magical Farolito Walk on Canyon Road. Luminarias, or farolitos, line the historic street, creating a warm and enchanting atmosphere. Galleries stay open late, and carolers serenade visitors, making it a festive and cherished tradition.

# INSIDER TIPS FOR ATTENDING
# LOCAL EVENTS

**Plan Ahead:** Many of Santa Fe's events and festivals draw large crowds, so planning is crucial. Check event schedules, purchase tickets in advance when possible, and consider making reservations for popular restaurants during special events.

**Explore Beyond the Main Events:** While the major events are highlights, do not overlook smaller, local gatherings and performances. Check out live music in intimate venues, attend gallery openings, and explore the diverse cultural events that may not be as widely advertised.

**Dress for the Weather:** Santa Fe's high-altitude desert climate means that temperatures can vary significantly throughout the day. Be prepared for warm days and cool evenings, especially in the spring and fall. Dress in layers and bring a hat and sunscreen for daytime events.

**Support Local Artists:** Whether attending art markets, film festivals, or music events, take the time to explore and support the work of local artists. Purchase unique souvenirs, engage with artists, and contribute to the city's vibrant creative community.

**Use Public Transportation:** Parking can be challenging during significant events, so consider using public transportation or rideshare services. This allows you to navigate the city without the stress of finding parking, especially in busy areas like the Plaza.

**Embrace Cultural Etiquette:** Respect traditions and etiquette for events with cultural or religious significance. Follow any guidelines organizers provide and be mindful of the cultural context to ensure a positive and enriching experience.

Santa Fe's events and festivals offer a dynamic tapestry of experiences, from culinary delights and film celebrations to cultural showcases and artistic expressions. By planning strategically, exploring beyond the main attractions, and embracing the unique cultural offerings, visitors can immerse themselves in the rich and diverse tapestry of Santa Fe's vibrant calendar of events.

# PHOTOGRAPHY AND MEMORY-MAKING

## PHOTO OPPORTUNITIES AND SCENIC SPOTS

**Historic Plaza:** Capture the heart of Santa Fe at the Historic Plaza. The adobe architecture, the Cathedral Basilica of St. Francis of Assisi, and the vibrant atmosphere make for iconic shots.

**Canyon Road:** Explore the art-lined streets of Canyon Road. Photograph the charming adobe galleries, outdoor sculptures, and the artistic spirit that permeates the area.

**Georgia O'Keeffe Museum:** Immerse yourself in the artistry of Georgia O'Keeffe. Photograph the museum's exterior and the beautiful sculptures in the surrounding landscape.

**Loretto Chapel:** Capture the enchanting spiral staircase inside the Loretto Chapel. The Gothic Revival architecture and intricate details provide stunning photographic opportunities.

**Santa Fe Opera House:** If visiting during the opera season, photograph the striking architecture of the Santa Fe Opera House against the backdrop of the Sangre de Cristo Mountains.

**Sunset at Cross of the Martyrs:** Hike to the Cross of the Martyrs for a panoramic view of Santa Fe. Capture the cityscape bathed in the warm hues of a Southwestern sunset.

**Bandelier National Monument:** Explore the ancient cliff dwellings and petroglyphs at Bandelier National Monument. Photograph the historical sites against the backdrop of the Frijoles Canyon.

**Turquoise Trail National Scenic Byway:** Drive along the Turquoise Trail and capture the high desert's scenic landscapes, adobe villages, and rustic charm.

## TIPS FOR CAPTURING THE ESSENCE OF THE DESTINATION

**Golden Hour Magic:** Embrace the golden hour—shortly after sunrise and before sunset—for soft, warm lighting that enhances the city's adobe architecture and landscapes.

**Cultural Details:** Focus on capturing the intricate details of Native American crafts, textiles, and art. Visit local markets and galleries to document the rich cultural tapestry.

**Street Photography in the Railyard:** Head to the Railyard Arts District for vibrant street scenes, colorful murals, and a dynamic blend of contemporary and traditional elements.

**Capture Local Festivities:** Attend local events and festivals to capture the lively spirit of Santa Fe. From traditional dances to contemporary art exhibits, these moments embody the city's dynamic culture.

**Explore Hidden Gems:** Wander off the beaten path to discover hidden gems. Explore lesser-known neighborhoods, art installations, and local cafes for unique photographic opportunities.

**Balloon Fiesta (October):** If visiting in October, capture the awe-inspiring sight of hot air balloons filling the sky during the Albuquerque International Balloon Fiesta, a short drive from Santa Fe.

**Adapt to Changing Light:** Santa Fe's high altitude means the light can change rapidly. Be prepared to adapt your camera settings to capture the varied lighting conditions, especially outdoors.

**Respectful Photography:** When photographing at Native American pueblos or during cultural events, be respectful and ask for permission. Some areas may have restrictions on photography to preserve sacred spaces.

**Document Seasonal Changes:** Return during different seasons to document the city's transformations. Each season, from blooming gardens in spring to snow-covered landscapes in winter, brings a new perspective.

**Capture Culinary Delights:** Do not forget to document your culinary adventures. Capture the colors and textures of iconic Southwestern dishes and the ambiance of Santa Fe's unique dining establishments.

Santa Fe offers a rich tapestry of photographic opportunities, blending natural beauty, cultural heritage, and artistic expression. By exploring the city with a photographer's eye and adapting to its diverse conditions, you will create a visual diary that captures the essence and spirit of the City Different.

# SAMPLE TINERARIES

3-DAY ITINERARY

Day 1: Cultural Exploration and Plaza District

**Morning:**

- Start your day at the Historic Plaza, the heart of Santa Fe. Explore the adobe architecture, visit the Cathedral Basilica of St. Francis of Assisi, and enjoy the vibrant atmosphere.

**Afternoon:**

- Have lunch at a local cafe near the Plaza.

- Spend your afternoon at the Georgia O'Keeffe Museum, appreciating the works of this iconic American artist.
- Stroll through Canyon Road, known for its art galleries showcasing diverse artworks.

**Evening:**

- Dinner in the Railyard Arts District, where various restaurants offer Southwestern and international cuisines.
- Consider catching a performance or live music at one of the local venues.

Day 2: Outdoor Adventures and History

**Morning:**

- Hike to the Cross of the Martyrs for stunning panoramic views of Santa Fe.
- Enjoy a hearty breakfast at a local spot.

**Afternoon:**

- Take a scenic drive to Bandelier National Monument to explore ancient cliff dwellings and petroglyphs.
- Have lunch in nearby Los Alamos.

**Evening:**

- Return to Santa Fe and relax with dinner at a restaurant featuring local flavors.

Day 3: Culinary Delights and Local Markets

**Morning:**

- Experience the Santa Fe Farmers' Market for fresh produce, local crafts, and a taste of the community.
- Have brunch at a nearby restaurant.

**Afternoon:**

- Take a Southwestern cooking class to learn about regional culinary techniques.
- Explore the city's art scene further by visiting more galleries or museums.

**Evening:**

- Enjoy a farewell dinner at a restaurant that highlights the diverse and delicious cuisine of Santa Fe.

This itinerary provides a mix of cultural exploration, outdoor activities, and culinary delights, allowing you to experience the unique charm of Santa Fe in a short period. Adjustments can be made based on personal interests and preferences.

## 5-DAY ITINERARY

Day 1: Cultural Immersion in Plaza District

**Morning:**

- Explore the Historic Plaza, visit the Cathedral Basilica of St. Francis of Assisi, and enjoy breakfast at a local cafe.

**Late Morning to Afternoon:**

- Dive into art at the Georgia O'Keeffe Museum and wander through the galleries on Canyon Road.
- Lunch at a restaurant in the Railyard Arts District.

**Afternoon to Evening:**

- Visit additional art galleries or museums in the Railyard area.
- Dinner in the Railyard Arts District.
- Attend a live performance or cultural show in the evening.

Day 2: Outdoor Adventures and Taos Excursion

**Morning:**

- Hike to the Cross of the Martyrs for panoramic views.
- Enjoy breakfast at a local spot.

**Late Morning to Afternoon:**

- Take a scenic drive to Bandelier National Monument for exploration.
- Have lunch in nearby Los Alamos.

**Afternoon to Evening:**

- Return to Santa Fe for a relaxed evening.
- Dinner at a local restaurant.

Day 3: Day Trip to Taos and Art Exploration

**Morning:**

- Full-day excursion to Taos. Visit Taos Pueblo and explore the historic Taos Plaza.
- Lunch at a charming Taos restaurant.

**Afternoon to Evening:**

- Explore Taos art galleries and boutiques.
- Return to Santa Fe for dinner.

Day 4: Relaxation, Spa, and Culinary Delights

**Morning to Afternoon:**

- Indulge in a spa day or wellness activities.
- Lunch at a cozy cafe or restaurant.

**Afternoon to Evening:**

- Explore additional art galleries or museums.
- Dinner at a high-end restaurant, savoring Santa Fe's diverse cuisine.

Day 5: Neighborhood Exploration and Culinary Experience

**Morning to Afternoon:**

- Explore neighborhoods such as Canyon Road, the Historic Plaza, and the Railyard Arts District.
- Visit local shops, boutiques, and art galleries.

**Afternoon to Evening:**

- Enjoy a late lunch at a neighborhood cafe.
- Attend any ongoing festivals or events.
- Dinner at a restaurant offering a unique and memorable culinary experience.

This 5-day itinerary provides a mix of outdoor adventures, cultural exploration, and culinary delights, allowing you to immerse yourself in the diverse offerings of Santa Fe.

Adjustments can be made based on personal preferences and the time of year.

7-DAY ITINERARY

Day 1: Historic Plaza and Cultural Exploration

**Morning:**

- Explore the Historic Plaza, visit the Cathedral Basilica of St. Francis of Assisi, and enjoy breakfast at a local cafe.

**Late Morning to Afternoon:**

- Dive into art at the Georgia O'Keeffe Museum and stroll through galleries on Canyon Road.
- Lunch at a restaurant in the Railyard Arts District.

**Afternoon to Evening:**

- Visit additional art galleries or museums in the Railyard area.
- Dinner in the Railyard Arts District.
- Attend a live performance or cultural show in the evening.

Day 2: Outdoor Adventures and Bandelier National Monument

**Morning:**

- Hike to the Cross of the Martyrs for panoramic views.
- Enjoy breakfast at a local spot.

**Late Morning to Afternoon:**

- Day trip to Bandelier National Monument for exploration.
- Lunch in nearby Los Alamos.

**Afternoon to Evening:**

- Return to Santa Fe for a relaxed evening.
- Dinner at a local restaurant.

Day 3: Day Trip to Taos and Art Exploration

**Morning:**

- Full-day excursion to Taos. Visit Taos Pueblo and explore the historic Taos Plaza.
- Lunch at a charming Taos restaurant.

**Afternoon to Evening:**

- Explore Taos art galleries and boutiques.
- Return to Santa Fe for dinner.

Day 4: Relaxation, Spa, and Culinary Delights

**Morning to Afternoon:**

- Indulge in a spa day or wellness activities.
- Lunch at a cozy cafe or restaurant.

**Afternoon to Evening:**

- Explore additional art galleries or museums.
- Dinner at a high-end restaurant, savoring Santa Fe's diverse cuisine.

Day 5: Neighborhood Exploration and Culinary Experience

**Morning to Afternoon:**

- Explore neighborhoods such as Canyon Road, the Historic Plaza, and the Railyard Arts District.
- Visit local shops, boutiques, and art galleries.

**Afternoon to Evening:**

- Enjoy a late lunch at a neighborhood cafe.
- Attend any ongoing festivals or events.
- Dinner at a restaurant offering a unique and memorable culinary experience.

Day 6: Art and History Immersion

**Morning to Afternoon:**

- Visit additional museums such as the New Mexico Museum of Art or the Museum of International Folk Art.
- Lunch at a restaurant featuring local flavors.

**Afternoon to Evening:**

- Explore historical sites like the San Miguel Mission and the Loretto Chapel.
- Dinner in the Historic Plaza area.

Day 7: Culinary Delights, Local Markets, and Farewell

**Morning to Afternoon:**

- Experience the Santa Fe Farmers' Market for fresh produce, local crafts, and a taste of the community.
- Have brunch at a nearby restaurant.

**Afternoon to Evening:**

- Take a Southwestern cooking class to learn about regional culinary techniques.
- Explore the city's art scene or revisit your favorite spots.

- Enjoy a farewell dinner at a restaurant that highlights the diverse and delicious cuisine of Santa Fe.

This 7-day itinerary allows a deeper exploration of Santa Fe's rich culture, history, and culinary scene. Adjustments can be made based on personal preferences, seasonal considerations, and special events during your stay.

## 14-DAY ITINERARY

### Day 1-3: Cultural Immersion in Historic Plaza District

### Day 1:

Morning:

- Explore the Historic Plaza.
- Breakfast at Tia Sophia's for their famous breakfast burritos.

Late Morning to Afternoon:

- Visit the Georgia O'Keeffe Museum.
- Lunch at The Shed for authentic New Mexican cuisine.

Afternoon to Evening:

- Stroll through Canyon Road galleries.
- Dinner at Geronimo, an upscale restaurant known for inventive cuisine.
- Attend a performance at the Lensic PAC.

**Day 2:**

Morning:

- Visit the San Miguel Mission and the Loretto Chapel.
- Breakfast at Cafe Pasqual's, known for its unique Southwestern flavors.

Late Morning to Afternoon:

- Explore the Palace of the Governors and the New Mexico History Museum.
- Lunch at The Plaza Cafe, serving contemporary Southwestern dishes.

Afternoon to Evening:

- Shop for souvenirs at the Palace of the Governors Portal.
- Dinner at Coyote Cafe, a contemporary Southwestern restaurant.

**Day 3:**

Morning:

- Explore the Randall Davey Audubon Center & Sanctuary for birdwatching.
- Breakfast at Chez Mamou French Bakery & Cafe.

Late Morning to Afternoon:

- Visit the Santa Fe Botanical Garden.
- Lunch at The Tea House for a light, garden-inspired meal.

Afternoon to Evening:

- Take a scenic drive along the Turquoise Trail.
- Dinner at The Compound Restaurant for upscale Southwestern cuisine.

## Day 4-5: Outdoor Adventures and Bandelier National Monument

**Day 4:**

Morning:

- Hike to the Cross of the Martyrs for panoramic views.
- Breakfast at Clafoutis, a French bakery with a local twist.

**Late Morning to Afternoon:**

- Day trip to Bandelier National Monument. Explore ancient cliff dwellings.
- Lunch at Pig + Fig Cafe in White Rock.

**Afternoon to Evening:**

- Relax and recharge back in Santa Fe.
- Dinner at La Choza for traditional New Mexican fare.

**Day 5:**

Morning:

- Explore the Tsankawi section of Bandelier National Monument for a less crowded experience.
- Breakfast at The Pantry for classic New Mexican comfort food.

Late Morning to Afternoon:

- Visit the Los Alamos History Museum.
- Lunch at Pajarito Brewpub & Grill.

Afternoon to Evening:

- Explore the Bradbury Science Museum.

- Dinner at Blue Window Bistro for eclectic cuisine.

**Day 6-7: Taos Exploration and Art**

**Day 6:**

Morning:

- Full-day excursion to Taos. Visit Taos Pueblo.
- Breakfast at Michael's Kitchen.

Late Morning to Afternoon:

- Explore the historic Taos Plaza.
- Lunch at The Gorge Bar & Grill.

Afternoon to Evening:

- Visit the Kit Carson Home & Museum.
- Dinner at the Love Apple.

**Day 7:**

Morning:

- Visit the Millicent Rogers Museum.
- Breakfast at Orlando's New Mexican Cafe.

Late Morning to Afternoon:

- Explore Taos art galleries and shops.
- Lunch at The Historic Taos Inn.

Afternoon to Evening:

- Return to Santa Fe.
- Dinner at Luminaria Restaurant & Patio for global flavors.

## Day 8-9: Relaxation, Wellness, and Culinary Delights

### Day 8:

Morning to Afternoon:

- Indulge in a spa day at Ten Thousand Waves.
- Lunch at Terra at the Four Seasons Resort.

Afternoon to Evening:

- Explore additional art galleries or museums.
- Dinner at Geronimo or Sazon for a memorable culinary experience.

### Day 9:

Morning to Afternoon:

- Attend a wellness workshop at the Santa Fe Institute of Natural Healing.

- Lunch at The Tune-Up Cafe.

Afternoon to Evening:

- Attend a live performance at The Lensic.
- Dinner at Restaurant Martín, blending French and Southwestern flavors.

## Day 10-11: Neighborhood Exploration and Culinary Adventure

**Day 10:**

Morning to Afternoon:

- Explore different neighborhoods - Railyard Arts District, Canyon Road, and the Historic Plaza.
- Lunch at Cafe Fina in the Railyard.

Afternoon to Evening:

- Attend any ongoing festivals or events.
- Dinner at Santa Cafe, known for its Southwestern-inspired dishes.

**Day 11:**

Morning to Afternoon:

- Explore the hip and artsy areas of the Railyard Arts District.
- Lunch at Modern General, a unique cafe and general store.

Afternoon to Evening:

- Attend a local art class or workshop.
- Dinner at Fire & Hops is a gastropub with a comprehensive craft beer selection.

## Day 12-14: Culinary Delights, Local Markets, and Farewell

## Day 12:

Morning to Afternoon:

- Experience the Santa Fe Farmers' Market for fresh produce, local crafts, and community vibes.
- Have brunch at The Guadalupe Cafe.

Afternoon to Evening:

- Take a Southwestern cooking class at the Santa Fe School of Cooking.
- Explore the city's art scene or revisit your favorite spots.

- Dinner at Radish & Rye for a farm-to-table dining experience.

**Day 13:**

Morning to Afternoon:

- Visit the International Folk Art Market if it aligns with your travel dates.
- Lunch at Jambo Cafe for a taste of African-Caribbean cuisine.

Afternoon to Evening:

- Attend a workshop or class at the Santa Fe School of Cooking.
- Dinner at TerraCotta Wine Bistro for a diverse menu.

**Day 14:**

Morning to Afternoon:

- Explore the local art markets and shops.
- Lunch at Sweetwater Harvest Kitchen for healthy, farm-to-table options.

Afternoon to Evening:

- Take a final stroll through the Historic Plaza.
- Enjoy a farewell dinner at Coyote Cafe Cantina.
- Attend a live music performance at a local venue for a perfect send-off.

This 14-day itinerary aims to provide a diverse and enriching experience in Santa Fe, with a mix of cultural immersion, outdoor adventures, wellness activities, and culinary delights. Adjustments can be made based on your preferences and the time of year. Enjoy your journey through the City Different!

# SUMMARY

Santa Fe beckons with its distinctive charm and cultural richness in the heart of the American Southwest. The city's unique offerings weave a tapestry of experiences that captivate visitors throughout the year. From the enchanting historic Plaza District, where centuries-old adobe structures echo tales of the past, to the vibrant Railyard Arts District, where creativity thrives in repurposed warehouses, Santa Fe invites exploration at every turn.

The annual events calendar, adorned with highlights like the Santa Fe Indian Market and the Farolito Walk on Canyon Road, showcases the city's commitment to celebrating its diverse heritage. Culinary adventures unfold during Santa Fe Restaurant Week, and the Film Festival illuminates the city with cinematic brilliance. Whether exploring the top-notch art galleries of Canyon Road or immersing in the rhythms of

Santa Fe Bandstand, each visit unfolds as a unique journey through the City Different's multifaceted identity.

While this guide offers a curated glimpse into Santa Fe's treasures, the true magic lies in venturing beyond its pages. Take a spontaneous detour through the lesser-known neighborhoods, where hidden gems await discovery. Engage with locals, savor unscripted moments in cozy cafes, and embrace the city's dynamic energy. Santa Fe's artistic soul extends beyond museums and galleries—immerse yourself in impromptu performances, local markets, and the warm hospitality of its residents.

Santa Fe, the City Different, invites you to immerse yourself in a world where tradition and innovation coexist harmoniously. As adobe walls stand testament to centuries of history, contemporary creativity breathes life into its streets. Whether indulging in culinary delights, navigating the diverse neighborhoods, or participating in the festivities that define each season, Santa Fe leaves an indelible mark on every visitor. Beyond the tangible allure of its landscapes and architecture, the city's intangible spirit beckons you to explore, engage, and savor the extraordinary blend of culture, art, and tradition that sets Santa Fe apart. Santa Fe's vibrant hues and cultural notes will resonate in the tapestry of your travel memories, inviting you to return to the City Different for another chapter of discovery.

As we reach the culmination of this journey together, I am filled with gratitude for the time you have invested in exploring the pages of this book. Your feedback is invaluable, and I invite you to share your thoughts with others by leaving a review on Amazon.

Your review has the power to guide potential readers, offering insights into the impact and value of this work. Whether you found inspiration, gained new perspectives, or enjoyed the narrative, your words can resonate with others seeking a similar experience.

Please take a moment to share your honest review on Amazon. Your feedback supports the author and helps build a community of readers who appreciate meaningful and thought-provoking literature.

Thank you for being an essential part of this literary journey. Your words matter, and your review can make a difference.

To Review On Amazon

# BIBLIOGRAPHY

*Canyon Road Arts – the complete visitors guide to arts, dining and the Santa Fe lifestyle.* (2016, June 23). Retrieved January 5, 2024, from https://canyonroadarts.com/

Kuyper, J. (n.d.). *Santa Fe Botanical Garden.* Retrieved January 5, 2024, from https://www.santafebotanicalgarden.org/

*Meow Wolf: Immersive Art Experiences.* (n.d.). Retrieved January 5, 2024, from https://meowwolf.com/

*New Mexico History Museum.* (n.d.). Retrieved January 5, 2024, from http://nmhistorymuseum.org/

*Santa Fe Institute.* (n.d.). Retrieved January 5, 2024, from https://www.santafe.edu/

*Santa Fe New Mexican | Santa Fe New Mexico daily news, sports, arts & culture news.* (n.d.). Retrieved January 5, 2024, from https://www.santafenewmexican.com/

*Santa Fe Opera.* (n.d.). Retrieved January 5, 2024, from https://www.santafeopera.org/

*Santa Fe Railyard.* (2023, March 31). Retrieved January 5, 2024, from https://www.railyardsantafe.com/

*Ski Santa Fe.* (2023, December 27). Retrieved January 5, 2024, from https://skisantafe.com/

*The Georgia O'Keeffe Museum.* (2024, January 5). Retrieved January 5, 2024, from https://www.okeeffemuseum.org/

*TOURISM Santa Fe.* (n.d.). Retrieved January 5, 2024, from https://www.santafe.org/

*Tripadvisor: Over a billion reviews & contributions for Hotels, Attractions, Restaurants, and more.* (n.d.). Retrieved January 5, 2024, from https://www.tripadvisor.com/

*Welcome to Santa Fe New Mexico | City of Santa Fe.* (n.d.). Retrieved January 5, 2024, from https://www.santafenm.gov/

# ABOUT THE AUTHOR

Kimberly Cordova, a native of La Crosse, Wisconsin, and raised in the vibrant landscapes of Denver, Colorado, currently calls the enchanting city of Santa Fe, New Mexico, home, where she resides with her husband, Greg.

Kimberly's life journey has been rich with diverse experiences. She spent most of her life as a dedicated single mother to her daughter, Channa. It was not until her late forties that she embarked on a new chapter, entering into matrimony with Greg. The couple shares their lives in Santa Fe, finding joy in the everyday moments.

Family holds a special place in Kimberly's heart. Her daughter, Channa, is married, and she has blessed Kimberly with two adorable grandchildren, Vera and Tillman. Kimberly affectionately refers to them as the "grandsugars" and considers them the treasures of her life.

While Kimberly's professional background spans multiple decades in the IT/Technology field, her true passions extend far beyond the confines of the digital world. An avid traveler, Kimberly has explored numerous countries, drawing inspiration from the diverse cultures and histories she has encountered.

In addition to her love for travel, Kimberly is a woman of many interests. She finds solace and joy in crochet, indulges her curiosity through trivia, and cherishes moments spent with family and friends. Her appreciation for the arts is evident in her love for live music and theatre, while a deep connection to nature fuels her spirit.

A self-proclaimed foodie, Kimberly delights in culinary adventures, exploring the world's diverse flavors. Her insatiable curiosity about history and other cultures has fueled her desire to learn continuously.

Kimberly's latest venture into writing is a testament to her pursuit of passion and a mid-life career change. She seeks to explore and share the depths of her experiences through her words, bringing to life the myriad interests that have shaped her remarkable journey.

Kimberly invites readers to join her on a literary adventure as she continues to evolve, discovering the beauty in life's varied tapestry.

amazon.com/author/kimberlycordova
linkedin.com/in/kimberlyburk

Made in the USA
Las Vegas, NV
18 March 2024

87403966R10075